FAVOURITE
SCOTTISH
RECIPES

compiled by
Johanna Mathie

*Keep gude company and ye'll
be counted one o'them.*
Scottish Proverb

SALMON

Index

Cover pictures *front:* Sheep shearing in the Highlands *by William Evans*
back: A Highland Spring Party *by John Frederick Taylor* PRWS

Printed and Published by J. Salmon Ltd., Sevenoaks, England © Copyright

Forfar Bridies

1 lb. Shortcrust pastry
12 oz. best stewing steak
1 medium onion, chopped finely

3 oz. shredded suet
¼ teaspoon mustard powder
Salt and pepper

Beaten egg to glaze

Set oven to 350°F or Mark 4. Chop the meat into very small pieces or mince coarsley. Place in a bowl with the chopped onion, salt, pepper and mustard. Sprinkle on the suet and mix well. Cut the pastry into 3 pieces and roll out each piece to a round about ¼ inch thick. Spoon the meat on to one half of each round, taking care not to overfill. Dampen the edges of the pastry, fold to make semi-circles and pinch the edges together to resemble small Cornish pasties. Place on a plain baking sheet. Brush with beaten egg and make a hole in each one for the steam to escape. Bake for about 1¼ hours until golden brown; if the pastry browns too quickly, cover with foil. Serve hot with vegetables or cold as a snack.

Oaty Crumbles

4 oz. self-raising flour   **2 oz. caster sugar**
½ teaspoon salt   **1 generous tablespoon golden syrup**
4 oz. rolled oats   **4 oz. butter or margarine**
Oatmeal for sprinkling

Originally, black treacle would have been used in this recipe.

Set oven to 350°F or Mark 4. Grease a 7 inch cake tin. Melt the sugar, syrup and butter in a saucepan and remove from the heat. Sift the flour and salt into a bowl and add the oats. Pour the cooled syrup mixture on to the dry ingredients. Mix well. Press the mixture into the cake tin and sprinkle with some oatmeal. Bake for 20 to 25 minutes until light golden brown. Mark into slices, allow to cool in the tin and then turn out and break up on a wire tray.

Clootie Dumpling

4 oz. self-raising flour	2 oz. soft brown sugar
2 oz. white breadcrumbs	1 tablespoon golden syrup
3 oz. shredded suet	½ oz. mixed spice
2 oz. sultanas	1 egg, lightly beaten
2 oz. currants	4 fl oz. milk

Grease a 3 pint pudding basin. Mix all the dry ingredients in a large bowl. Stir in the egg, syrup and milk to make a soft consistency. Fill the basin with the mixture, leaving plenty of room for the pudding to swell. Cover with a layer of greaseproof paper buttered on both sides and cover and seal with kitchen foil. Place on a heatproof plate in a large saucepan. Fill the pan with water halfway up side of the basin. Cover and simmer for 2 hours. Top up with boiling water as necessary. Turn out onto a large plate. Serve with warm syrup and whipped cream. Serves 4.

This pudding would traditionally have been made in a cloth or "clout" – hence the name Clootie Dumpling.

Cocky Leeky Soup

1 small chicken and giblets (2½ –3 lb.)	1 small carrot, grated
1 onion, chopped	1 teaspoon salt
6 leeks, cut into inch long pieces	3 pints water
2 oz. long grain rice	Salt and pepper
	1 tablespoon chopped parsley

Place the chicken, giblets and onion in a large saucepan. Add the water and bring to the boil. Cover and simmer for 1½ hours until the chicken is tender. Remove from the heat and skim off any white scum. Take out the giblets and discard. Take out the chicken and strip the meat from the bones. Discard the bones. Return the meat to the stock. Add the leeks, rice and grated carrot. Bring back to the boil, cover and simmer for a further 30 minutes. Season with salt and pepper to taste. Add the parsley before serving. Serves 4-6.

Poached Salmon with Green Mayonnaise

6 salmon cutlets   Cucumber, sliced for garnish

COURT-BOUILLON
**2 pints water   1 cup white wine   1 carrot, chopped   1 onion, chopped
2 sticks celery, chopped   Bay leaf   Salt and pepper**

MAYONNAISE
**2 eggs   ½ pint olive oil   1 teaspoon salt   1 teaspoon mustard powder
Pepper to taste   Dash wine vinegar   Freshly chopped parsley and chives to taste**

Put all the bouillon ingredients together in a saucepan. Simmer for 30 minutes. Strain and replace the liquid in the pan. Add the salmon, bring to the boil and boil for 2 minutes. Remove from heat and set aside; the salmon will continue to cook in the bouillon while you make the mayonnaise. Put the eggs in a food processor or blender with the mustard, salt and pepper. Switch on and whilst blending, pour in the oil and vinegar in a steady stream until the sauce thickens. Add the chopped herbs. Check that the salmon is cooked (10-12 minutes). Lift on to a serving dish. Garnish with sliced cucumber and serve hot or cold with the mayonnaise.

Glen Lussa by E. W. Haslehust R.I

Shortbread

4 oz. butter   **6 oz. flour**
2 oz. caster sugar   **2 oz. ground rice**

Set oven to 350°F or Mark 4. Cream the butter and sugar together in a bowl. Gradually sift in the flour and the ground rice, kneading the mixture into a ball. On a floured surface roll or pat the dough into a round, ½ inch thick. Place on a plain baking sheet. Pinch up the edges and prick the top with a fork. Bake for about 35-40 minutes or until firm and pale golden. While still warm, cut into triangles and sprinkle with caster sugar.

Scotch Woodcock

4 slices buttered toast or	**2 tablespoons milk**
4 slices fried bread	**Small pinch of salt**
1 oz. butter	**Pepper**
4 eggs	**Anchovy fillets**

Make the toast and butter it or fry the bread. Keep warm. Melt the butter in a saucepan. Stir in the eggs and milk, season and cook over a gentle heat, stirring continuously, until the mixture thickens. Spoon the eggs on to the toast and top with anchovy fillets. Delicious as a light supper.

Sweet Mutton Hot Pot and Dumplings

1½ lb. neck of mutton or lamb
2 teaspoons redcurrant jelly
2 onions, chopped
3 carrots, chopped

1 turnip, chopped
6 oz. mushrooms, sliced
1 parsnip, chopped and blanched
1 tablespoon tomato purée

1 pint vegetable stock or water

DUMPLINGS
4 oz. self-raising flour   2 oz. shredded suet   1 teaspoon chopped parsley

Set oven to 375°F or Mark 5. Put the pieces of meat in the bottom of a large casserole. Spread them with the redcurrant jelly and place in the oven for 15 minutes. Remove and add the chopped vegetables and a little salt and pepper. Stir the tomato purée into the stock or water. Pour over the meat and vegetables. Return to the oven. Reduce the heat to 350°F or Mark 4 and cook for about 1½ hours until the meat is tender. Dumplings: mix together the flour, suet, parsley and seasoning with enough water to form a stiff dough. This should make about six small dumplings. Add the dumplings to the hot pot for the last 30 minutes of cooking. Serve with buttered, mashed potatoes and a green vegetable. Serves 4-6.

Hard Sauce for Plum Puddings

4 oz. butter   **1 tablespoon brandy**
4 oz. sugar   **2 tablespoons ground almonds**

1 drop of almond essence can be used instead of the ground almonds.

Cream the butter and sugar together in a bowl and then gradually beat in the brandy and the ground almonds. Put into a serving dish and refrigerate until required. This sauce can be served with any kind of steamed plum or fruit pudding.

Aunt Mary's Plum Pudding

4 oz. self-raising flour   4 oz. currants   4 oz. raisins   4 oz. breadcrumbs
4 oz. dark brown sugar   4 oz. shredded suet
1 large apple, peeled, cored and chopped
½ teaspoon mixed spice   ½ teaspoon cinnamon   ½ teaspoon nutmeg
2 eggs   Juice and rind of a lemon   4 tablespoons rum   1 cup milk

Grease a 2 pint pudding basin. Mix all the dry ingredients together in a large bowl. Add the eggs, lemon and rum and sufficient milk and stir well to produce a dropping consistency. Put the mixture into the basin. Cover with a circle of greased paper and kitchen foil or a pudding cloth and steam for 3 hours. If the pudding is to be kept for a while before eating, steam for a further 3 hours before using. Serve with Hard Sauce. Serves 6.

Roast Grouse

Brace of young grouse, plucked and drawn   Giblets
2 oz. butter   6 rashers streaky bacon
2 slices white bread (crusts removed)
2 tablespoons redcurrant jelly   Salt and pepper
Watercress to garnish

Set oven to 400°F or Mark 6. Rub a little of the butter into the well-washed and dried inside of each bird. Spoon the redcurrant jelly into the cavities. Season the outside of the grouse. Cover the breasts with bacon rashers. Place in a roasting tin and cover with foil. Allow 15 minutes per pound plus an additional 15 minutes. Meanwhile toast the bread. Place the giblets in saucepan, cover with water and simmer until tender. Strain and reserve the stock to make the gravy. Remove the livers, mash them with butter, salt and pepper and spread on the toast. Slip the toast under each bird for the last 15 minutes of roasting. Place the grouse and toast on a serving dish and garnish with watercress. Serve with game chips, redcurrant or rowan jelly and bread sauce.

Red Grouse by George Rankin

Rowan Jelly

Rowan berries   Sugar   Water

Pick and wash the berries. Put them in a large, heavy saucepan or preserving pan and just cover with water. Simmer gently. When the berries will crush with a wooden spoon the fruit is ready for straining. Strain through a jelly bag, or a nylon sieve double lined with gauze. Add 1 pound of sugar each to 1 pint of juice. Boil until setting point is reached, usually about 30-40 minutes. Test for setting on a cold plate. When ready, pour into small pots, cover and allow to set. This jelly is especially delicious with game.

Scotch Broth

1 lb. neck of mutton or lamb
2½ pints water
1 small turnip, chopped
1 leek, chopped
1 large carrot, chopped

1 small carrot, grated
1 onion, chopped
1 oz. cabbage, shredded
1 oz. pearl barley
Chopped parsley to garnish

Place the meat in a saucepan with the water. Add the pearl barley. Season with salt and pepper. Bring to the boil, cover and simmer for 1 hour. Skim off any white scum. Add the chopped vegetables, cover and simmer for another 1 hour, adding the grated carrot and the cabbage for the final 30 minutes of cooking. Before serving remove the meat and bones, and discard the bones. The meat can be returned to the broth or eaten separately, if preferred. Bring back to the boil and serve, garnished with chopped parsley.

Porridge

2 pints water or 1 pint water and 1 pint milk
5 oz. porridge oats   Pinch of salt

Bring the water, or milk and water to the boil in a saucepan; add the oats. Stir briskly to avoid lumps. Simmer with the lid on for 10 minutes. Remove from the heat. Add the salt, replace on the heat and cook for a final 10-15 minutes. Serves 4.

Traditionally porridge would be served with separate bowls of double cream. Each spoonful of porridge is then dipped into the cream before eating. For an extra treat sprinkle with sugar and whisky.

Cranachan

1 pint double cream   3 tablespoons clear honey (heather honey is best)
3 tablespoons whisky   4 tablespoons thick, plain yoghurt
1 oz. fine oatmeal   6 oz. raspberries

Toast the oatmeal in a pan under a hot grill until golden. Set aside to cool. Put the cream, honey and whisky in a bowl and whip together until it forms peaks. Fold in the yoghurt. Spoon the mixture into a serving dish and chill in the refrigerator for 2 to 3 hours. Before serving, sprinkle the oatmeal over the mixture and pile the raspberries in the centre. Serves 6.

Ideally Cranachan should be made with Crowdie, a soft Scottish cheese but yoghurt makes a good substitute.

Oatmeal Bannock

6 oz. flour	1 oz. butter
2 oz. medium oatmeal	1 teaspoon baking powder
1 level teaspoon salt	¼ pint milk
1 oz. caster sugar	

To test for the correct heat of the girdle sprinkle it with a little flour.
If the flour browns at once it is too hot; it should take a few seconds to turn colour.

Sift the flour, salt and baking powder into a bowl. Add the butter and rub into a fine consistency. Gently mix in the oatmeal and the sugar. Make a well in the centre. Gradually pour in the milk, stirring the mixture lightly with a wooden spoon until it forms a sticky soft dough. Turn on to a lightly floured surface, and knead very gently (handle as little as possible). Roll out lightly and shape into one or two ½ inch thick rounds. Heat a girdle or heavy bottomed frying-pan, and sprinkle with a little flour to prevent sticking. Cook for about ten minutes on one side. When the underside is brown turn once only and cook other side. Cool on a wire rack. Slice thinly and serve with butter and jam.

Collops of Beef

1½ lb. piece of braising steak, sliced into 4   1 onion, chopped
6 oz. mushrooms, sliced   2 tablespoons flour
2 oz. butter   Salt and freshly ground black pepper
Bayleaf (optional)   ¾ pint beef stock

Set oven to 350°F or Mark 4. Mix the flour with the salt and pepper. Coat the beef slices with seasoned flour. Melt the butter in a frying pan. Fry the collops for about 2 minutes on each side. Remove from the pan and set aside. Gently fry the onion and the mushrooms. Put the onion and mushrooms and a bayleaf (if desired) into a casserole. Lay the collops on top. Pour in the stock, cover and cook for 1½ hours. Serve with buttered mashed potatoes and a green vegetable. Rowan or redcurrant jelly goes well with this dish. Serves 4.

Collops of beef are traditionally served on Burns Night.

Highland Cattle by H. Jamieson

Scotch Egg

12 oz. pork sausagemeat   2 teaspoons parsley, finely chopped
4 eggs   1 oz. flour, seasoned with salt and pepper
1 egg, beaten   4 oz. dried breadcrumbs

Vegetable oil for deep frying

Boil the eggs for 10 minutes. Cool and remove the shells. Place the sausagemeat in bowl. Add the chopped parsley and mix well; hands are best. Coat the eggs with the seasoned flour and cover completely with a layer of sausagemeat; wet hands help to mould it evenly. Dip into the beaten egg and roll in the breadcrumbs. Fry in deep fat until golden brown. Drain well on kitchen paper. Serve hot or cold. Serves 4.

Treacle and Marmalade Tart

8 oz. shortcrust pastry   **4 oz. marmalade**
8 oz. golden syrup   **8 oz. white breadcrumbs**
2 tablespoons lemon juice

Set oven to 350°F or Mark 4. Roll out the pastry, and line an 8 inch flan dish. Trim the edges and reserve the extra pastry. Sprinkle the breadcrumbs evenly over the pastry base. Warm the syrup and marmalade very gently in a saucepan over a very low heat. Stir in the lemon juice. Pour the mixture over the breadcrumbs. Roll and cut the left-over pastry into thin strips and make a lattice pattern over the tart. Cook for 25-30 minutes until golden brown. Serve hot or cold with whipped cream. Serves 6.

Stovies

3 tablespoons vegetable oil or dripping   1 medium onion, sliced
1½ lb. potatoes   Salt and pepper
6 oz. left-over cooked meat or 2 oz. grated cheese

Put the fat in a heavy bottomed saucepan and fry the onion gently for 2 to 3 minutes. Peel the potatoes, slice thickly and add to the pan with a little salt and pepper. Cover and cook very gently for about an hour until the potatoes are cooked through. Remove from the heat. Stir the mixture of onions and potatoes then pile on to a warm serving dish. Serve with slices of cold cooked meat. As an alternative, sprinkle the mixture with cheese and brown under a hot grill. A good simple supper dish.

The Old Pier, Lamlash, Isle of Arran by Alexander Cameron

Cullen Skink

1 large Finnan haddock	1 pint full cream milk or buttermilk
1 onion, chopped	1 oz. butter
½ lb. mashed potato	Salt and pepper

Place the haddock in a large pan with sufficient water to cover. Bring to the boil, add the chopped onion and simmer for 10-15 minutes until the fish is cooked. Remove the fish, retaining the stock, and flake the flesh from the bones and skin. Set the flesh to one side and return the bones and skin to the stock. Boil for 30 minutes. Remove from the heat and strain the stock into a clean pan. Add the flaked fish and return to the heat. Add the milk and salt to taste and bring to the boil for a few minutes. Stir in the mashed potato, butter and pepper to taste, and serve immediately. Serves 4.

A hearty fisherman's soup traditionally always made with Finnan haddock.

Creamy Finnan Haddie

2 Finnan haddocks (divided into 4 pieces)
1 pint milk   2 oz. butter   2 tablespoons flour
2 heaped teaspoons dry mustard
5 fl oz. double cream   Bayleaf   Pepper

Finnan Haddies have a lovely subtle flavour ideal for this dish; other smoked haddock, however, can be substituted, if necessary.

Place the fish in a large saucepan. Cover with the milk. Add the bayleaf and pepper. Bring to the boil. Reduce heat and simmer gently until the fish is cooked. Carefully lift the fish with a slice, drain and place in a heated shallow serving dish; cover with foil and keep warm. Strain the fish milk into a jug. Melt the butter in a saucepan. Stir in the flour and mustard. Cook for 2 minutes. Add the fish milk. Bring to the boil, stirring continuously until it thickens. Remove from the heat. Stir in the cream. Reheat the sauce but do not boil. Pour over the fish. Serve with boiled potatoes and a fresh green vegetable. Serves 4.

Parlies Scottish Parliament Cakes

8 oz. flour   4 oz. butter or margarine   2 oz. caster sugar
2 tablespoons golden syrup or black treacle
1 teaspoon ground ginger (optional)   1 large egg

Originally black treacle would have been used in this recipe.

Set oven to 350°F or Mark 4. Grease a baking tray. Cream together the butter and sugar in a mixing bowl. Add the flour, the egg and the syrup (together with the ginger, if required.) Beat well. Alternatively, put all the ingredients in a blender and mix well but ensure that they are at room temperature. Drop dessertspoonfuls on to the baking tray leaving room for them to expand. Bake for 15-20 minutes until light golden brown. Place on a wire rack to cool.

A delicious cross between a cake and a biscuit.

Loch Achray and Ben Venue by A. de Breanski Jnr.

Green Tomato and Apple Chutney

2 lb. green tomatoes, skinned and chopped
2 lb. cooking apples, cored and chopped
1 lb. onions, peeled and finely chopped
4 oz. sultanas   4 oz. raisins
½ oz. ground ginger   12 oz. brown sugar
1 tablespoon dry mustard powder   1 teaspoon salt
1 pint vinegar (wine or malt)

Prepare the tomatoes, apples and onions, leaving the skin on the apples. Place in a saucepan with all the other dry ingredients. Add the vinegar. Bring to the boil over a gentle heat. Stir until the sugar dissolves. Simmer gently for about 2 hours, stirring from time to time. When cooked put into clean, warm jars and cover with vinegar-proof tops. Keep in a cool place.

Mutton Pies

HOT WATER CRUST
**8 oz. flour   2 oz. lard or vegetable fat   2 fl oz. milk
2 fl oz. water   Pinch salt   1 egg yolk**

FILLING
**12 oz. lean mutton or lamb   6 tablespoons meat stock, gravy or water
Salt and pepper**

As a variation, add some chopped onion, mushroom and parsley to the filling.

Make the filling first. Chop the meat finely and season. Set aside. Set oven to 375°F or Mark 5. Sieve the flour and salt into a bowl. Boil the lard, water and milk together in a saucepan. Make a well in the flour and pour in the hot mixture: mix well with a knife and knead until smooth. Roll out two thirds of the paste on a floured surface, keeping a third for lids. Cut into 6 circles and press into deep patty tins. Spoon the meat into each tin, moistening each filling with a spoonful of stock, gravy or water. Cut the remaining dough into 6 smaller circles for lids. Brush the edges with water and seal. Make a split in each pie lid to allow steam to escape. Brush with egg yolk. Cook for 30-40 minutes. Serve hot or cold.

S/ Lamona Bird

Queen Mary's Tart

8 oz. puff pastry   **2 oz. butter**
2 tablespoons jam   **2 oz. chopped mixed peel**
2 oz. sugar   **1 tablespoon sultanas**
2 eggs, beaten

Set oven to 425°F or Mark 7. Roll out the pastry on a floured surface and line a 7 inch greased flan dish. Spread the jam over the pastry base. Melt the sugar and butter in a saucepan over a very gentle heat. Add the mixed peel and sultanas. Remove from the heat and mix in the beaten eggs. Pour into the pastry case. Bake for 20-25 minutes until the filling is set and golden brown. Serve hot or cold as a pudding with whipped cream or cold, sliced, as a tea-time treat.

Butterscotch Meringue Pie

8 oz. shortcrust pastry	2 oz. flour
4 oz. light soft brown sugar	¾ pint milk
3 oz. butter	2 egg yolks
1 tablespoon water	3-4 drops vanilla essence

TOPPING
2 egg whites   3 oz. caster sugar
1 level tablespoon granulated sugar

Set oven to 350°F or Mark 4. Roll out pastry and line an 8 inch flan dish. Bake blind for about 20 minutes. Put 1 oz. butter in saucepan and add sugar and water. Heat gently until the sugar dissolves. Do not boil. Set aside. In a second saucepan melt remaining butter. Add the flour and stir. Add the milk. Bring to the boil, stirring well. Boil for 5 minutes. Stir in the caramelised sugar from the first saucepan. Allow sauce to cool before adding the egg yolks and vanilla essence. Beat them in well. Pour into the cooked pastry case. Reduce oven to 325°F or Mark 3. Topping: put egg whites into a clean bowl. Beat until they form stiff peaks. Fold in the caster sugar with a metal spoon. Pile meringue on top of pie and sprinkle with granulated sugar. Bake for 20 to 30 minutes until meringue is pale golden.

Howtowdie

1 chicken, approx. 3½ lb.   1 pint chicken stock   2 oz. butter   1 chicken liver, chopped
8 baby onions or shallots   2 tablespoons double cream   2 whole cloves
Salt and pepper to taste   Pinch of nutmeg   1 lb. spinach

STUFFING
2 oz. breadcrumbs   ½ teaspoon tarragon   1 teaspoon chopped parsley
1 small onion, chopped   Milk to bind

Set oven to 350°F or Mark 4. Wash the chicken thoroughly inside and out. Prepare the stuffing by adding sufficient milk to the breadcrumbs to make them swell. Stir in the herbs and onion and mix thoroughly. Stuff the chicken and secure. melt the butter in a large, heavy based casserole, on the stove and add the onions to soften. Place the chicken in the casserole and brown. Add the cloves, nutmeg and a little salt and pepper and pour in the stock. Cover and cook in the oven for 1½ hours. Remove the chicken from the casserole and keep warm. Strain the stock into a saucepan, add the liver and cook gently. At the same time cook the spinach and drain well; season to taste. Mash the liver well into the stock and stir in the cream.

To serve: arrange a bed of spinach on an oval platter, place the chicken in the centre and pour the sauce over.

Thirty-Nine

Skirlie Stuffed Chicken

A 3-3½ lb. chicken
4 oz. medium or coarse oatmeal
1 medium onion, chopped
2 oz. shredded suet or 2 oz. dripping
Salt and pepper
Mixed herbs (optional)

Set oven to 350°F or Mark 4. Remove the giblets for the gravy. Rinse and wipe the chicken well. Put the oatmeal, onion and the suet or dripping into a bowl. Add salt, pepper and herbs to taste. Mix well with a fork. Stuff the chicken. Take care not to overfill the cavity as the oatmeal swells when cooked. Place the chicken in a roasting tin and roast for about 20 minutes to the pound and possibly 20 minutes over depending on the bird. Serve with roast potatoes and fresh vegetables. Serves 4.

A versatile dish, Skirlie was often eaten instead of meat, especially when times were hard. Here it makes a delicious stuffing.

Torrisdale Bay, Kintyre by E. W. Haslehurst R.I.

Partan Bree – Crab Soup

1 large boiled crab   **1 pint milk**
3 oz. long grain rice   **¼ pint single cream**
1 pint chicken stock   **½ teaspoon anchovy essence**
Salt and pepper

Remove all the meat from the crab and set aside the flesh from the large claws. In a pan boil the rice in the milk until soft but take care not to over cook. Add the crab meat, (except from the claws), and rub the mixture through a sieve into a clean pan. Bring to the boil gradually, stirring in the chicken stock. Remove from the heat and add the anchovy essence, the meat from the claws and salt and pepper to taste. Reheat but do not boil, stir in the cream and when hot serve immediately. Serves 4.

Whisky and Chocolate Crunch

6 oz. chocolate digestive biscuits, crushed
1 pint whipped cream
3 tablespoons whisky
1 oz. caster sugar

2 egg whites
2 drops vanilla essence
1 oz. toasted split almonds
Grated chocolate to decorate

Crush the biscuits and spread equal amounts in the bottom of six glass sundae dishes. Whip together in a bowl the cream, whisky, sugar and vanilla until stiff. In a separate bowl whip the egg whites until stiff, then fold into the cream mixture. Spoon equal quantities of the mixture into the dishes, covering the biscuits. Chill and decorate with toasted almonds and grated chocolate.

Auntie Ellen's Winter Warmer

½ bottle whisky **½ lb. clear honey**
½ lb. caster sugar **⅓ pint sweet cider**
Small bottle of rosehip syrup

Mix the sugar, cider, honey and rosehip syrup together in a large bowl. Add the whisky and stir thoroughly for a few minutes. Bottle and store in a cool place. If rosehip syrup is unavailable then any fruit syrup will suffice. The quantities can be reduced in proportion if required. Scottish Heather Honey is preferable. A delicious sweet and potent drink.

Oaty Vegetable Soup

½ oz. butter
1 medium carrot, chopped
1 medium turnip, chopped
1 medium onion, chopped
1 leek, trimmed and chopped

1 oz. medium oatmeal
1 pint of meat or vegetable stock
¾ pint milk
Salt and pepper
Chopped parsley

Melt the butter in a large saucepan. Add the vegetables and sweat in the butter over a very gentle heat, with the lid on, for 5 minutes. Stir in the oatmeal and cook for a further few minutes. Pour in the stock and stir well. Bring to the boil, then reduce the heat and simmer, covered, for 45 minutes. Add the seasoning and the parsley. Finally add the milk, reheat gently, and serve piping hot. Serves 4.

Black Bun

8 oz. flour
1 lb. currants
1 lb. raisins
2 oz. chopped mixed peel
4 oz. caster sugar
4 oz. chopped blanched almonds
¼ pint milk
1 level teaspoon ground cinnamon
1 level teaspoon ground ginger
½ teaspoon ground allspice
Pinch ground cloves
Pinch ground black pepper
½ teaspoon bicarbonate of soda
1 tablespoon brandy
12 oz. shortcrust pastry
Beaten egg for glazing

Set oven to 350°F or Mark 4. Mix the flour, bicarbonate of soda, spices and sugar in a bowl. Add the raisins, currants, mixed peel and almonds. Moisten the mixture with the milk and brandy and stir well. Roll out two-thirds of the pastry to line a well greased 10 inch cake tin. Fill with the fruit mixture and make a lid with remaining pastry. Seal the edges using a little cold water; press firmly. Brush with beaten egg. Finally make four holes with a skewer right to the bottom of the tin. Bake for 2-2½ hours; the cake is ready when a skewer pushed in comes out clean. If the top is browning too much, protect with greaseproof paper. Cool, slice and serve.

This festive cake is traditionally eaten at Hogmanay.

METRIC CONVERSIONS

The weights, measures and oven temperatures used in the preceding recipes can be easily converted to their metric equivalents. The conversions listed below are only approximate, having been rounded up or down as may be appropriate.

Weights

Avoirdupois	Metric
1 oz.	just under 30 grams
4 oz. (¼ lb.)	app. 115 grams
8 oz. (½ lb.)	app. 230 grams
1 lb.	454 grams

Liquid Measures

Imperial	Metric
1 tablespoon (liquid only)	20 millilitres
1 fl. oz.	app. 30 millilitres
1 gill (¼ pt.)	app. 145 millilitres
½ pt.	app. 285 millilitres
1 pt.	app. 570 millilitres
1 qt.	app. 1.140 litres

Oven Temperatures

	°Fahrenheit	Gas Mark	°Celsius
Slow	300	2	150
	325	3	170
Moderate	350	4	180
	375	5	190
	400	6	200
Hot	425	7	220
	450	8	230
	475	9	240

Flour as specified in these recipes refers to plain flour unless otherwise described.